KAWAII:
HOW TO DRAW REALLY
CUTE
FANTASY
CREATURES

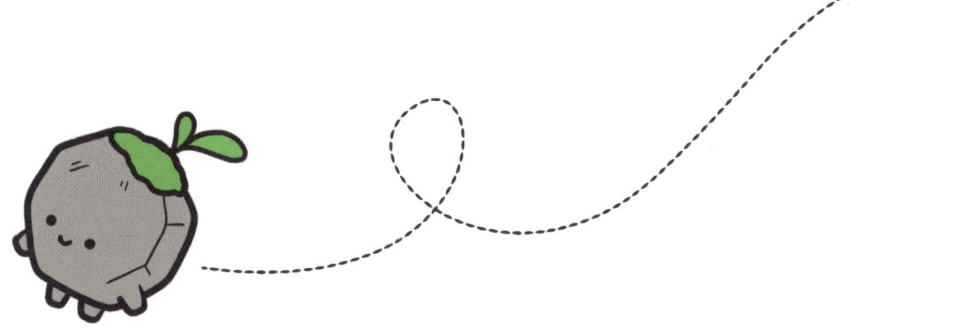

This book belongs to:

....

....

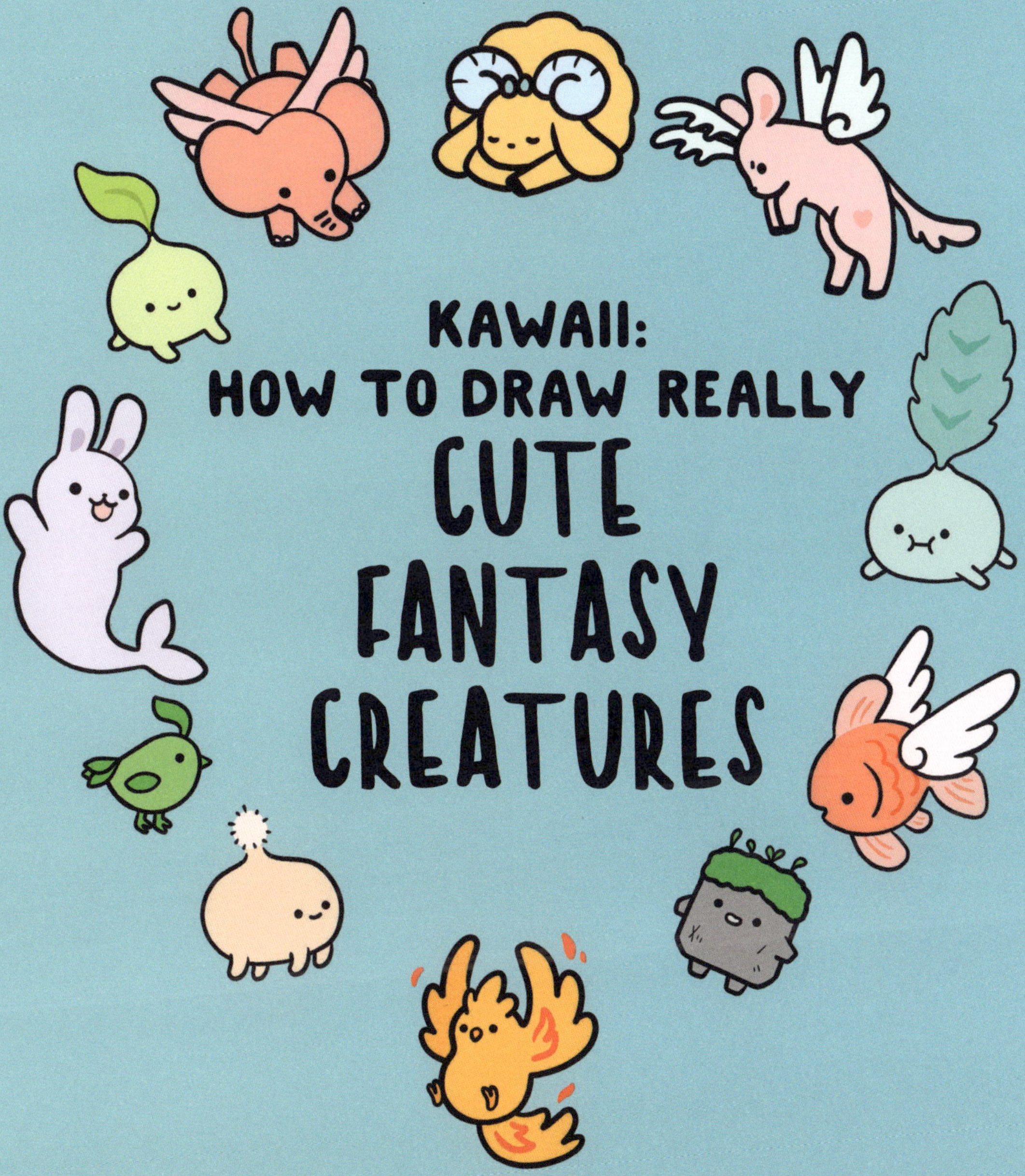

KAWAII:
HOW TO DRAW REALLY
CUTE
FANTASY
CREATURES

Angela Nguyen

Search Press

This edition published in 2020 by

Search Press Ltd
Wellwood
North Farm Road
Tunbridge Wells
Kent TN2 3DR
United Kingdom

Reprinted 2021, 2022, 2023 (twice), 2024, 2025

Copyright © 2019 Quarto Publishing plc

An imprint of The Quarto Group

ISBN 978-1-78221-908-8

Conceived, edited and designed by
Quarto Publishing plc
1 Triptych Place,
Lodon, SE1 9SH,
United Kingdom
www.quarto.com

QUAR.336379

Editor: Claire Waite Brown
Designer: Karin Skånberg
Senior Art Editor: Martina Calvio
Publisher: Samantha Warrington

Printed in Guangdong Province, ChinaTT092025

CONTENTS

Hi there, my name is Angela!

I'm an artist who likes to draw animals and cute things.
I love that making cute art always brings happiness to others.
There's just something about the simplicity of being able to
make a doodle that brings joy into another person's life.
I hope this is something that you also enjoy doing!

In this book I have brought together a collection of mythical
creatures. Some of them you may know, as they appear in
familiar legends and stories, while other creatures will be
new to you because I made them up! I'm excited for us
to draw these creatures together, and even to teach you how to
make your own. Let's explore the soon-to-be-discovered wonders
of these critters in their water, sky and land homes.

ANGELA NGUYEN

Chapter one
SETTING THE SCENE

You don't need special tools, materials or skills to draw fantasy creatures. Grab your pens and paper, then learn how to give your drawings cute appeal! You can also have some fun creating worlds for your fantastic beasties to live and play in.

TOOLS AND SURFACES

There are many types of tools you can use to draw and colour cute fantasy creatures. These are some of the tools that I love to use.

You can pick up any piece of paper and draw a creature on it.

Try not to drop coloured pencils because the lead inside will break.

How cute is this unicorn pencil topper?

CRAYONS

If you're going to be doing a lot of colouring, crayons can be a fun tool to play with. They make interesting textures and thick strokes.

The pencil is a go-to!

PENCILS

Pencils are ideal for sketching and creating fun textures. Pencil marks are also easy to erase.

Metallics
add sparkle!

SURFACES

You don't need special paper; any kind of drawing surface is just fine. If you want to keep all your drawings together, you could use a sketchbook, or a simple notebook will do.

Sticky notes are fun to draw on. You can stick them anywhere and everywhere!

There's no going back with a pen.

PENS

These are my favourite! Pens are great when you want a thin stroke. You can get precise markings, perfect facial expressions or pattern details.

MARKERS

Markers can be a bit risky because they are ink-heavy, so test them out first. I have some markers in my office that are light and create beautiful thick strokes.

Sharpies define lines.

Use art markers for rich colour and vibrancy.

BEASTLY BEGINNINGS

There are as many fantasy beasts to draw as your imagination can conjure up. Thankfully, there are just a few simple techniques you need to know to get started.

Three fundamental shapes

The three shapes you need to draw any fantasy creature are the circle, square and triangle. Each shape can be drawn longer, thinner, fatter, larger or smaller to create any other special shapes!

Simply squish a circle to draw an oval.

Lengthen a square, vertically or horizontally, and you have a rectangle.

Lengthen a triangle, or make it curvy, to draw wings, or ears, or other creature parts.

The fundamental shapes making up the pegasus are squashed circles and elongated squares. Its body is a jelly-bean shape, which is an oval with an extra squish on one side.

Jelly-bean shape

Circles and ovals

Squares and rectangles

The pterodorkyl is all about the triangles.

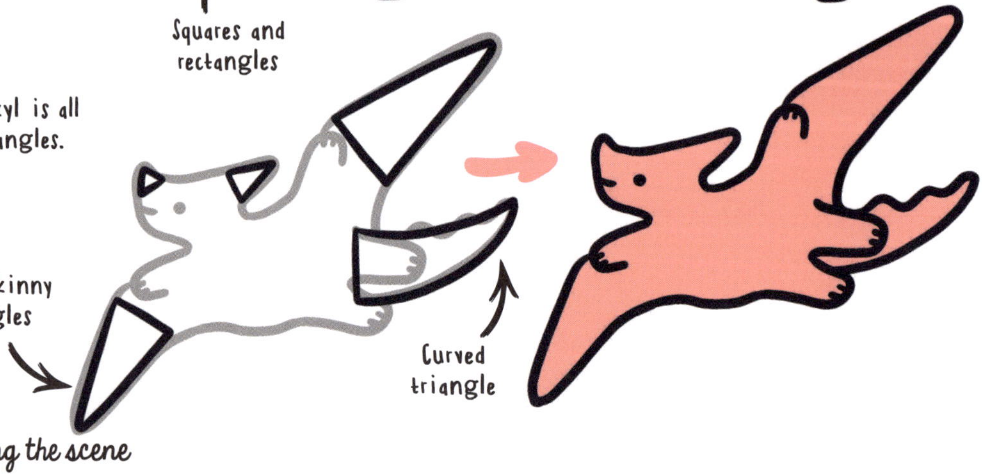

Long, skinny triangles

Curved triangle

The three fundamental shapes are combined to create the creature's base. The base helps you set up your drawing when you're starting out.

This is the base of an alazard. It consists of two ovals and a curved triangle.

The next stage is to join up the shapes and add on any extras, such as limbs and facial details.

When you have your new creature, erase the base because you don't need it anymore!

Even when your creature changes its pose, the base will still be made up of the fundamental shapes. Always start with your base, and don't worry about the details until later.

MAKING THEM CUTE

It's easy to make fantasy beasts cute,
even monsters and dragons!

RULE 1: SIMPLIFY

Focus less on details and instead
use fewer lines and simple strokes.
The cute dragon doesn't have claws
or extra horns on its head.

RULE 2: ROUND LINES

Round lines and shapes make your
creature look soft and friendly.
Notice that the cute dragon's
wings and horns are rounded.

RULE 3: LIGHT AND BRIGHT

The final step to making your
character cute is colouring in the
lines with light or pastel colours.
You can also use bright colours
to create a cheery mood.

By changing facial expressions and adding
action lines next to your creatures you can give
life to your beasts and clearly communicate how
they are feeling.

HAPPY
A simple, happy face!

FUNNY
A smile and upward
eyebrows.

ANGRY
A frowny face, slanted
eyebrows and a puff
of steam.

SAD
Upward eyebrows
and an upside-down
mouth.

SCARED
Upward eyebrows,
open mouth with
extra lines and water
droplet symbols.

MISCHIEVOUS
Crooked eyebrows and
a bold smile.

SURPRISED
Open mouth, lifted
eyebrows and
expression lines.

DANGEROUSLY CUTE
One tooth poking out.

BORED
Straight eyebrows and
a slanted mouth.

PLAYFUL
Closed eyes and tongue
sticking out.

WORRIED
Upward eyebrows with
a frowny face.

BASHFUL
Upward eyebrows,
a blush and a heart.

WATER WORLDS

Watery homes for creatures include oceans, rivers and lakes, so water worlds can be drawn in many forms. Defining features are loose lines, cool colours and organic shapes.

This background is primarily made up of a large square with smaller triangles on top.

In the middle, make a wavy line for the start of the waterfall. Fill in the sides of the waterfall.

At the bottom of the waterfall draw a cloud shape to represent the watery foam.

Setting the scene

The ocean is a vast canvas that is home to many sea creatures. Experiment with a horizontal background where the water stretches out to the sides of the page.

Another aquatic background is a wavy river. Rivers run through bodies of land, so don't forget to include some grassy borders.

Shapes can mould the scene around your creature. Take this circle, for example: it created a lake! Surround the lake with plants and mountains.

SKY BACKDROPS

Creatures of the sky are not bound by anything! Recognizable skies are usually blue with puffy clouds, but other designs include sunsets, warmer colours, swirly textures and misty shapes.

A simple shape can make an amazing backdrop for your creature. Begin here with a circle.

Draw in clouds on opposite sides and overlapping the circle edges.

Erase the lines you don't need, like the circle behind the clouds.

Traditional clouds are known for their
puffy, candyfloss shapes. Draw swirls
around clouds to make them extra fluffy.

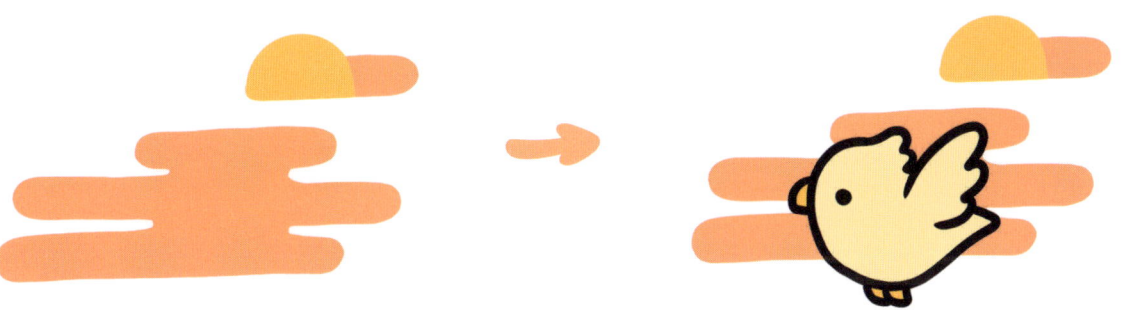

Use warm colours for a sky to create a sunset. These rounded horizontal
shapes are more abstract cloud forms, and adding the semicircle
makes it seem like the sun is peeking out from behind them.

Making a swirl is a cool way to
reshape puffy clouds. Add shadows
in between the layers in order
to create depth.

LAND LOVERS

If your fantasy beast dwells on land, you might include features such as mountains, trees, plants and grass in your drawings. Natural-looking scenery and landscape colours look good, but you can play around with different colours, and maybe even invent some new plants!

For a tree-lined mountainside scene, start with a box and add triangles on top.

Add more triangles inside the box. These will transform into trees.

Add more little triangles to form the tree details. Complete the scene with curvy lines for the foreground hills and rounded corners on the mountains.

Give your landscapes three-dimensionality by adding
a sky. Here's an example of a lowland grass scene,
with clouds added to suggest distance and height.

A background can be as simple as a few decorations
sprinkled around your creature. Just some leaves,
speckles and dots make a home for your beast.

Backgrounds can be drawn as platforms
for your creatures to stand on. Play around
with colour to create interesting moods.

MEET THE MENAGERIE

Some of the fantasy creatures I draw are from mythology, some are animal hybrids and others have popped straight out of my imagination. Here they all are for you to see, and choose which one you want to draw first!

--- *Water beasts* ---

NESSIE
28

SEAPONY
30

KRAKEN
32

BUNNY OCEANA
34

SHELGGIE
36

FLIPPER-FLAP FISH
38

GHOST WHALE
40

KHALEEL
42

LONG-LEG AL
44

GOLDEN DRAGON
46

TENTAGON
48

SOAREPHANT
52

FLOATING PUFFBALLS
54

ALAZARD
56

FLYION
58

CLOUD DRAGON
60

GRIFFIN
62

PEGASUS
64

ELEMENTAL BIRD
66

FLOOFY BAT
68

GHOST OWL
70

FLABBIT
72

HUMONGO FUZZ
74

PTERADORKYL
76

WINGEDEER
78

Land beasts

BASILISK — 82

RHINO PUP — 84

FIRE PUPPER — 86

PLUMASAUR — 88

UNICORN — 90

SKULL PUPPY — 92

LERRY — 94

ANTEON — 96

CELESTIAL CAT — 98

ROCK FELLA — 100

SHIBARUS — 102

FLORUS 104

OTTREE 106

ARMOURTAUR 108

SCALIA 110

GOOP MONSTER 112

FLOPPY RAM 114

ANTABUR 116

HORNED TIGER 118

Chapter two
WATER BEASTS

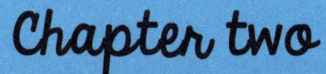

Prepare to be amazed as you discover the fantastic creatures that live in the rivers, swamps, lakes and oceans of the world.

NESSIE

A nessie is a shy water creature that likes to chill among the seaweed. Although it is bright pink, it is difficult to spot because it swims fast and is good at playing hide-and-seek.

Underwater backdrops are fun to draw because you can be loose with your lines! Draw wavy horizontal lines to give the watery effect.

Start by drawing a circle for the head and an oval for the body.

Connect the head and body with curved lines to make the neck, and add some flippers.

The finishing touches are the head fins and a tail.

Starting with the head and body makes it easier to visualize the rest of the nessie's body.

The direction of the neck determines which way the nessie is facing.

Nessie and friends

The nessie may be shy, but still enjoys swimming with its little fish friends.

SEAPONY

The seapony is a free-spirited creature that likes racing in the ocean. Sometimes it has dreams about galloping on land.

Circles, circles and more circles for the start of your seapony.

Join the circles up and add details all around them.

Give your creature's background an interesting shape. This one is circular with water dripping away at the bottom.

Draw the head circle and body oval close to one another when the seapony is turning its neck.

Galloping along

The seapony gallops in a similar way to a horse on land, just with two legs instead of four. Draw its body horizontally instead of upright.

Rearing up

Notice how the tail curves around the oval of the body. Use the oval as your guide for drawing the neck, too.

KRAKEN

The kraken is a giant octopus that lives in the darkest parts of the ocean. It appears at the surface of the water when it wants to hug a ship!

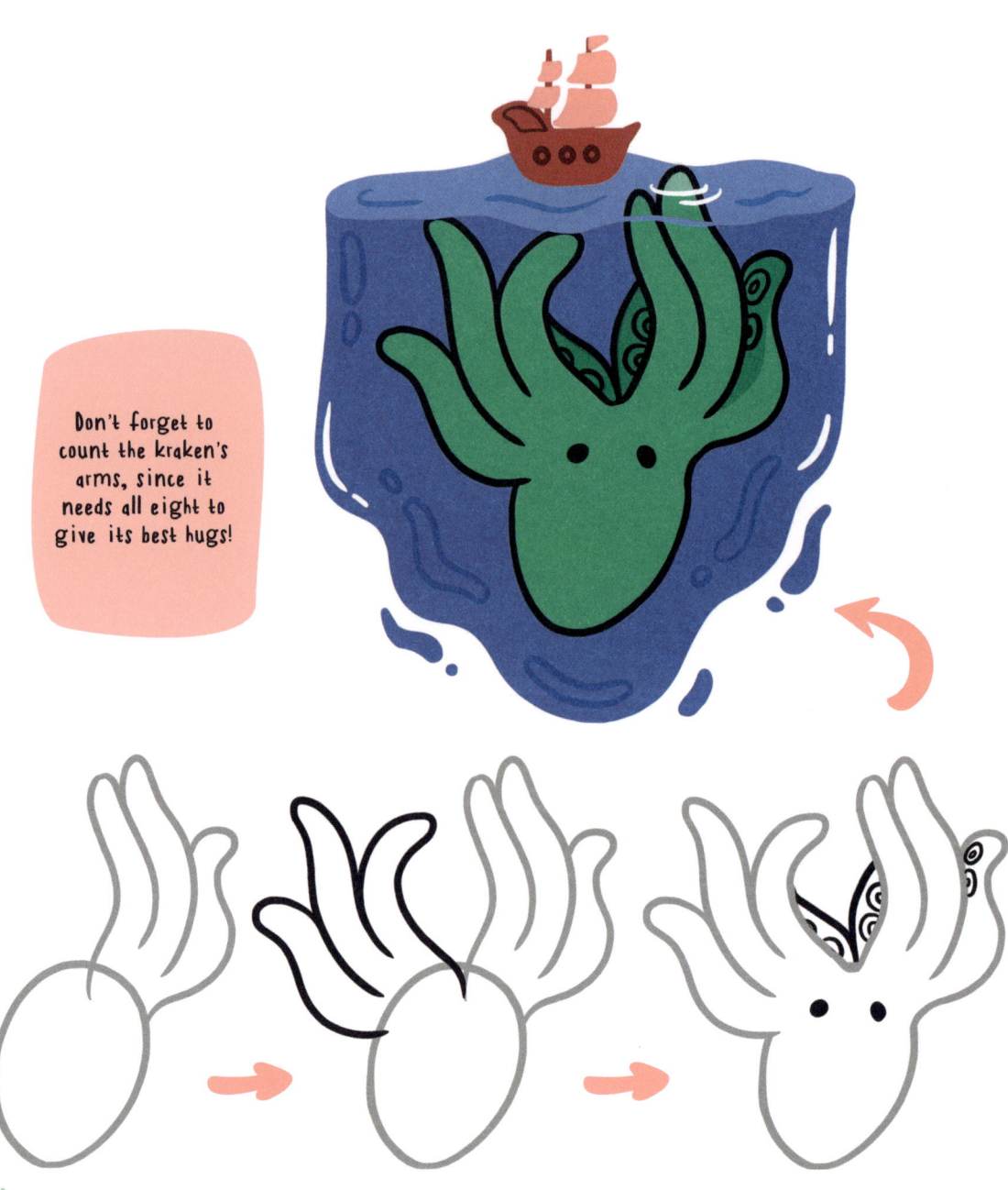

Don't forget to count the kraken's arms, since it needs all eight to give its best hugs!

Swimming on by

The head is not a regular oval, but is lopsided instead; one end is large while the other end is small.

Check out those tentacles on the inside of the arms.

A friendly wave

The arms can really inform the emotion of the kraken. This one looks friendly because it's waving!

Angry expression

Draw the oval head and start with some lines for the beginnings of the arms.

Continue to draw out the arms. They are bent and look a bit angry.

Add black puffs to show just how angry the kraken is!

BUNNY OCEANA

This water rabbit is a cute creature that lives inside a giant shell. It's very expressive: you can often tell how it's feeling by its ears.

The key to making the bunny oceana so animated is its soft features. The face and body are round, and the ears and tail parts are also curved.

Bunny paddle

When the bunny oceana is swimming, draw its head and body horizontally.

Use the round face and body as a guide to filling in the rest of the features.

Celebration pose

When this bunny's arms and tail are up, it's ready to celebrate!

Expressions

When its ears are halfway down, the bunny is shocked!

Ears up with puff symbols show that it's angry.

Lowered ears with a rain cloud means the bunny oceana is super sad.

SHELGGIE

The shelggie is a long-legged, long-necked turtle, with a spiky head and shell designed to protect it from scary monsters.

The shelggie swims with its head above the water. Colour the underwater body darker than the bits that peek out into the air.

Water beasts

Begin by drawing circles for the head and body and joining them up with curved lines for the neck.

Add the legs and draw rings where these, and the neck, connect to the body.

Finish with the shell pattern and spikes.

Snoozing

When drawing a sleeping shelggie, curve the neck so the head rests close to the body.

The shelggie's legs are tucked inside its shell, so only draw the rings this time.

FLIPPER-FLAP FISH

This special fish flaps its wings under water to swim. Since this fish also uses its flippers, it swims faster than the average fish.

Draw a large oval for the body and add smaller ovals for the fins.

Add a large, triangular oval extending from the body. This is the wing. Draw a few extra lines on the fins.

Add feathered details to the wing, then draw in a second wing and a final fin at the back, for super propulsion.

Begin with a large circle and add smaller ovals for the fins.

This is the downward action of the flapping wings.

Draw the wings upward to show the complete swimming motion!

Add skinny ovals for the wings.

Fishy cousin

Just by changing the body shape you can make a whole different design.

Instead of a circle, you can try drawing a longer oval for the body.

GHOST WHALE

The spooky ghost whale has its skeleton on show, and swims around on top of the water with its ghostly friends.

Start the ghost whale by drawing the body. Then slowly add the skeleton.

The skeleton may look difficult, but it's easy if you draw the bones one by one.

Start with the curved outline of the spine.

Outline each section and square.

Add lines to section off the spine.

Draw small squares on top of each section.

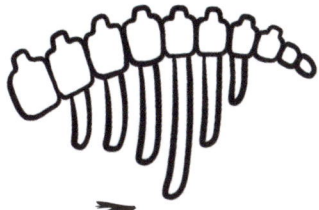

Add more long bones to the bottom of the spine.

The skeleton is like a puzzle that fits inside the ghost whale. When you add the skeleton, make sure it doesn't touch the creature's outline.

Resting weary bones

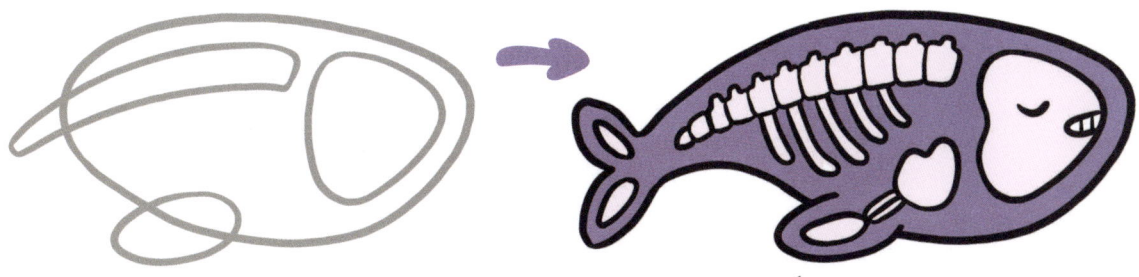

When the ghost whale sleeps, its tail and fins lie flat and its eyes close.

KHALEEL

The khaleel is a water eel with pincer claws.
Its squiggly body allows it to dance
all around the seaweed.

The khaleel has a
smooth triangular
head . . .

. . . with curved lines
for the tail and fins,
and to connect all the
elements together.

Draw some simple squiggly lines before you draw your eel. Use these to sketch different positions for the khaleel.

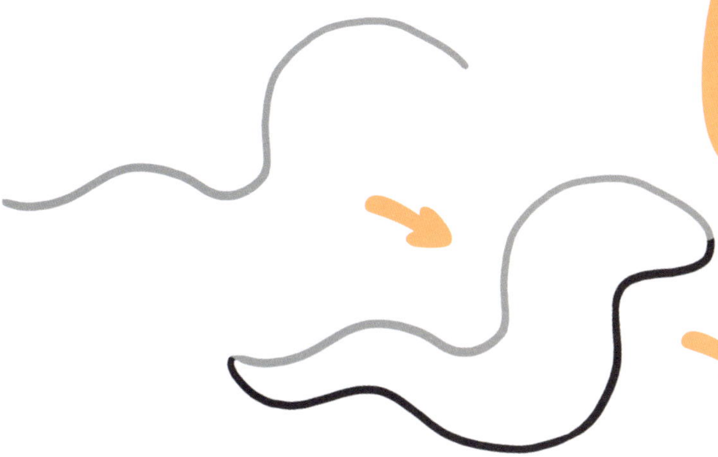

Look at how this drawing starts with a simple line and then slowly becomes the slithery creature.

Twisted spiral

When the khaleel is twisted, its body is like a spiral.

Khaleel 43

LONG-LEG AL

A long-leg al is the most friendly swamp creature you'll ever meet. Its long legs allow it to walk above the water and greet everyone that passes by.

The tufts of grass in the swamp are like little hearts!

This sketch looks like a banana!

Add long legs to the banana body.

Finish off with details, like the spikes on its back.

What's that noise?

Draw three ovals: a small one for the snout, a medium one for the head and a large one for the body.

Add the legs and tail, which extend from the body. Shape the snout and add some back ridges.

Colour your long-leg al in your favourite shade of green.

Naptime

Shhh, the long-leg al is sleeping. Draw the ZZZ symbol and its eyes closed to show that it is resting.

A little stroll

Sketch the body and the beginnings of the legs.

The other two legs point in the opposite direction as the beastie walks along.

Long-leg al **45**

GOLDEN DRAGON

The golden dragon doesn't breathe fire, but it can breathe both underwater and on land. It spends its days in the ocean collecting gold shells that match its skin.

There are a lot of shapes that make up the golden dragon, such as circles and ovals for the head and body, rectangles for the limbs and rounded triangles for the fins.

Begin with the head and body . . .

... then add horns and limbs that extend from the circles.

When colouring the golden dragon, bear in mind that the skin is a dark gold while the fins are lighter.

Sitting pretty

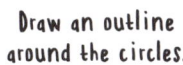

Draw the head stacked on top of the body.

Draw an outline around the circles.

Add in details, such as the little lines on the fins.

Golden dragon **47**

TENTAGON

The tentagon is a combination of an octopus and a dragon. It lives in the sea, occasionally coming up to the surface to look for shells.

First, draw a circle and oval. Then draw in the limbs near the bottom of the oval.

Draw in the octopus face and dragon wings.

The last steps are to draw in the details of the wings, and the fins on the head.

Happy dance

When the tentagon is happy, all its limbs join in the dance, including the tentacles on the face.

Flying

You can draw three different wing poses to show the tentagon flying.

Standing proud

When the tentagon is standing up, its body is like an oval.

The wings have a triangular shape to them.

Colour the wings slightly darker than the rest of the body.

Chapter three
BEASTS OF THE AIR

You'll be surprised at how many animals can fly in fantasy worlds. Even enormous elephants can take off.

SOAREPHANT

Although elephants are heavy, the soarephant has no problem soaring through the sky with its powerful wings.
It loves to fly during sunsets when the sky is pink.

As with most of the creatures you draw, start with circular shapes for the head and body.

Add the ears and limbs, not forgetting the cute trunk.

The wing is like an elongated rectangle, to which you can add feathery details.

To draw the soarephant facing you, start with the head, trunk and ears.

Draw the body and legs below. Add eyes and lines on the trunk.

Add the final touch of the wings facing downward. They're resting!

Sad baby

A simple way to show emotions is by using the ears and wings. By drawing them pointing downward, the soarephant appears sad.

Soaring on high

Start with the head, adding ears and a trunk.

Continue with the body and limbs lying flat out.

The wings are also flat out, because the soarephant is in full soaring mode.

FLOATING PUFFBALLS

Floating puffballs are a colony of colourful creatures that float in flocks. They can have different things on their backs, such as wings, plants or puffs.

Floating puffballs like to fly together. You can draw them in a single-file line, or all bunched up.

The puffball starts with a slightly squashed circle.

Next, draw the limbs and beginnings of the back.

Add a face and the back detail last of all.

Draw dashed lines and colour the centre of the back detail for a puffy effect.

Some puffballs are smaller than others.

What a big leaf! Sometimes the leaves are even bigger than the puffballs.

This puffball has wings on its back.

Triple puffball

This puffball has more than one shape on its back . . .

. . . for three little plants!

You can also draw the bodies with ovals instead of circles.

ALAZARD

The alazard is a winged lizard that, when not flying, likes to roam around mountains and forests. Its lizard friends prefer the hot desert, so the alazard spends a lot of time alone.

The alazard is an introverted animal, so it doesn't mind being alone. You'll always find it with a happy smile on its face.

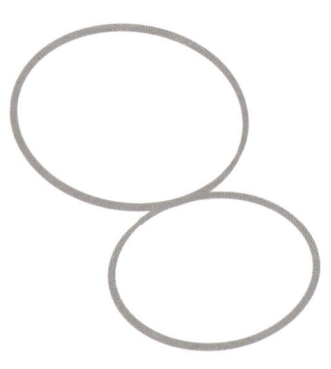

Start with two large circles stacked on top of one another. The head circle is the bigger one.

Connect the circles by drawing in the neck, and then add the limbs.

Finish off with wings and a tail.

The alazard's head is always bigger than its body.

Draw the wings above the body. Add an eye.

The alazard has tiny wings for such a heavy body.

Personality

You can draw your alazard with teeth by adding small white triangles to its mouth.

Another way to add some personality is with a silly tongue.

Trotting along

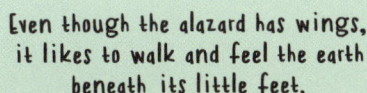

Even though the alazard has wings, it likes to walk and feel the earth beneath its little feet.

FLYION

The flyion is a fabulous creature. When it opens its wings, pink sparkly dust appears, announcing that this lion is ready to soar.

Draw pink sparkles around the flyion to show how fabulous it is.

Add rounded triangles for the wings, then make them feathery.

Draw a circle for the head, overlapped with an oval for the flyion's body.

Mane event

An easy way to draw the flyion's flower mane is to start with four semicircles, spacing them more or less equally around the head.

Complete the mane with four more semicircles.

Add the body, tail and wings to complete the drawing.

Sleepy flyion

When the flyion is sleeping it folds down its front legs and wings.

Add a ZZZ symbol to show that it mustn't be disturbed.

Cheeky wink

To draw a cheeky flyion, start with the body and head as usual . . .

. . . draw in the legs and mane . . .

. . . and finish with an upturned tail and wings, and a winking eye.

CLOUD DRAGON

This curious creature flies high in the sky, but it can be hard to spot because it likes to play hide-and-seek in the clouds.

Start out with a line that will guide the body of your dragon.

Fill in the rest of the body around the first line.

Draw in details like the back fins and little arms.

Snakelike form

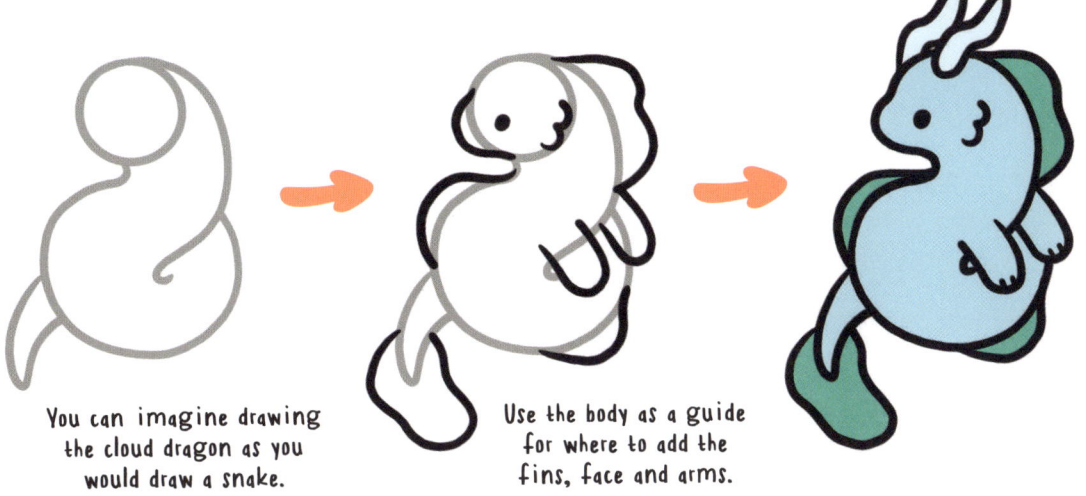

You can imagine drawing the cloud dragon as you would draw a snake.

Use the body as a guide for where to add the fins, face and arms.

Floaty flight

When it's flying the cloud dragon looks like a cute noodle. Draw the arms hanging down to exaggerate the curving motion.

An upward glance

Start with a snake body and a circle for the head.

Add in the details one at a time. Take it easy, you can do it!

Cloud dragon

GRIFFIN

The griffin is a mythical creature with a bird-like head and lion's body. It is bold and courageous, but also approachable.

To create this cool background, draw a triangle, then overlap it with oval clouds.

Make a circle head and oval body. Then draw in the limbs and bird's head around the shapes.

The last step is drawing the triangular wings and long tail.

Start with the base of the griffin, which is the circle head, oval body and rectangle legs.

Erase any extra lines you have and fill in the drawing with a solid colour.

Next, draw the head and triangular wings. Don't forget to add in the small lines on the legs and a tail.

Drawing wings

z z z z

The basic wing shape is a triangle. Add feather lines to complete the look. The wings can fan upward or downward.

Wings upward

Wings downward

PEGASUS

This creature has large, powerful wings that can fly it across the world. When travelling short distances, however, it prefers to run on land.

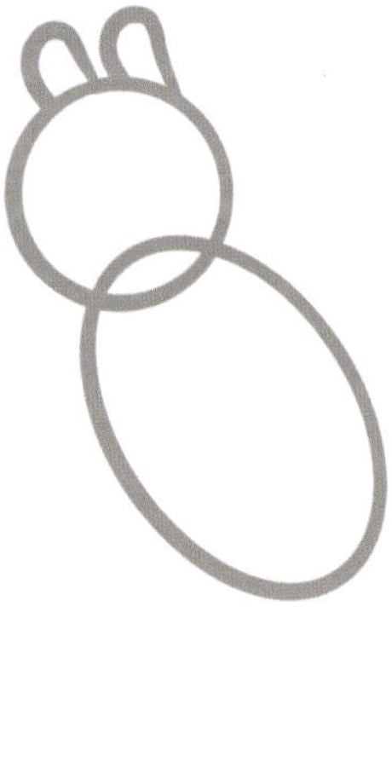

The base of every horse is a circle head and oval body. Add ears at this stage, too.

The next step is to draw repeating shapes. Notice how the legs are repeating lines. Even the mane and tail look similar.

Draw two triangle shapes for the wings.

Resting wings

Make the base of your horse by drawing the body, legs and head.

For this resting pose, draw an oval for the wing.

Draw in the wing feathers to complete the look, and add a mane.

Power poses

For an airborne gliding pose, draw the wings fanning out from both sides of the body.

To indicate motion in your drawing, draw a wavy line to show that the pegasus is bouncing forward.

Pegasus **65**

ELEMENTAL BIRD

Elemental birds are small friends with big special powers. Each bird has a different element that makes them unique.

For the fire element, make the feathers wavy and use warm colours.

The first step in making your creature is to draw a simple bird.

Once you have your bird, you can add in its elemental nature.

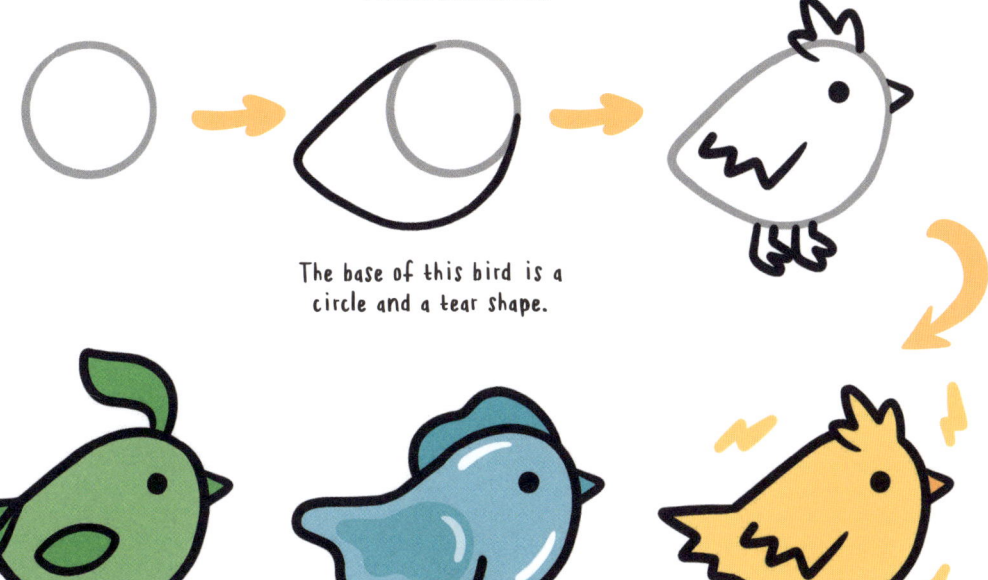

The base of this bird is a
circle and a tear shape.

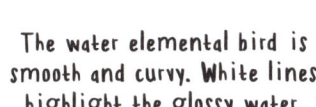

The nature elemental bird
is green in colour, with leaves
for feathers.

The water elemental bird is
smooth and curvy. White lines
highlight the glossy water.

The electric elemental bird
has spiky qualities and a
bright yellow colour.

Phoenix

The phoenix is an iconic fire bird.
Draw flames coming from the body
to make your bird extra spicy.

FLOOFY BAT

The floofy bat is unique because it has a fluffy coat and a poofy tail. Like most bats, it comes out at night, looking for fruit to snack on.

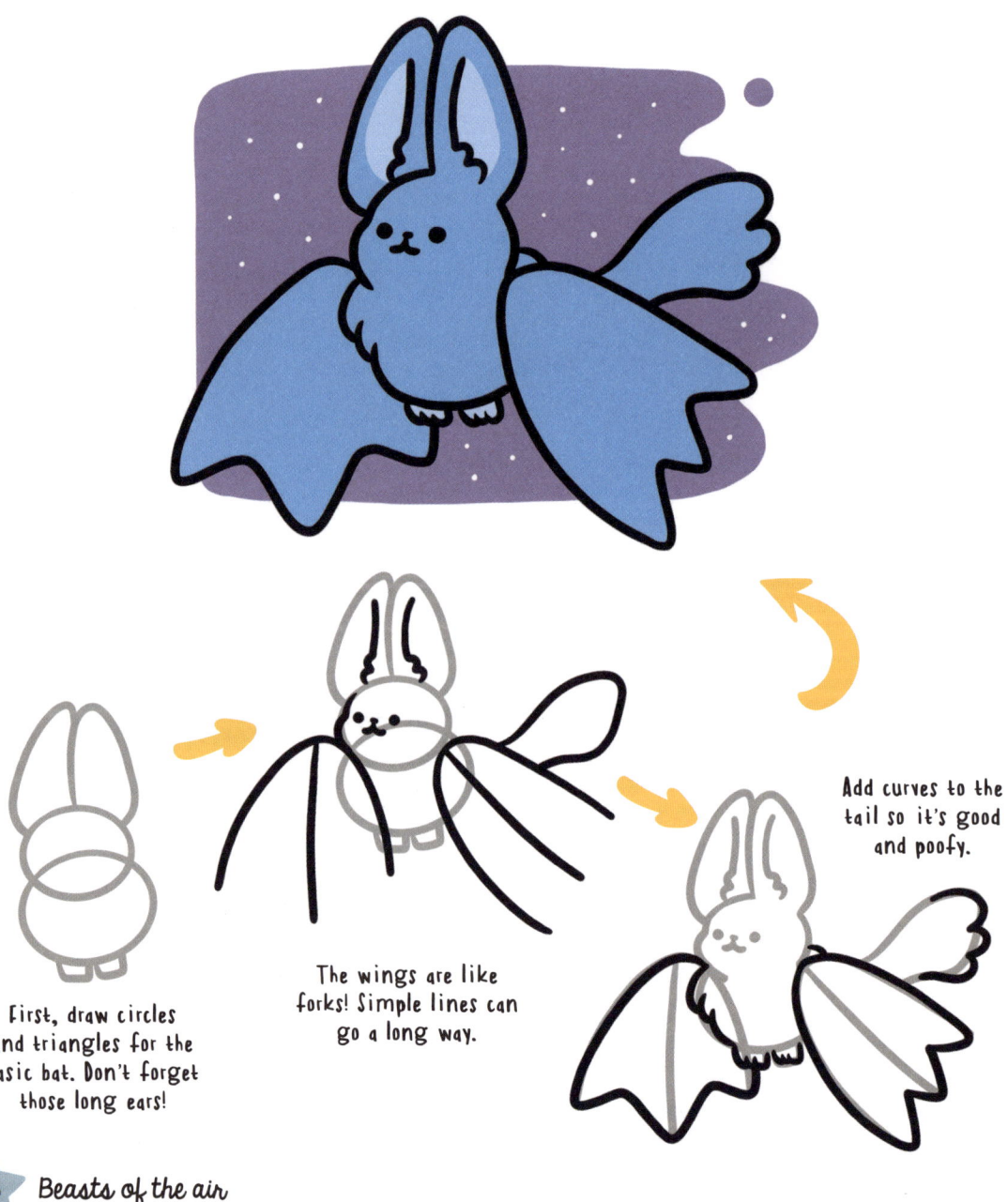

First, draw circles and triangles for the basic bat. Don't forget those long ears!

The wings are like forks! Simple lines can go a long way.

Add curves to the tail so it's good and poofy.

The floofy bat likes to sleep hanging upside down, with its wings wrapped around its body like a blanket.

You can make one wing fan out like a fork, while the other wing folds in like a triangle.

Fruity snack

The floofy bat loves sweet snacks, like sugary oranges. It grabs a piece of fruit in its feet and carries it home to munch on.

GHOST OWL

The only thing really spooky about the ghost owl is its skull face, because underneath it is a sweet friend.

An easy but cool background to draw is a circle with stars! Make the ghost owl overlap the circle, so it's not all the way in.

The body of the ghost owl is an egg shape. Hard boiled!

The tail is like a fun triangle with weird corners.

See how the mouth has a small curve to it.

The finishing touches are the feathery details around the wings, tail and head.

Swooping in

The swooping pose starts with a jelly-bean body and angular wings.

Add in feathers around the body, wings and tail.

Now your owl is ready to swoop into action!

Standing legs

For this pose start the legs with single lines . . .

. . . then build leg shapes around the lines. Put in all the feathery curved lines as well.

Curious

The curious pose has the ghost owl leaning over to one side.

You only need to draw one wing here; the other wing is tucked in at the back.

FLABBIT

A flabbit is a flying bunny with large, floppy ears. One flap of the ears can send the bunny high into the sky!

This flabbit is riding on a cloud! To make a riding cloud, draw a bubbly cloud with a wavy tail.

Make the ears about the same size as the body. Oh yes, they're big.

Draw the legs and arms hanging down near the bottom of the body.

Draw in the fluff of the ears. The same shapes can be applied to the tail and nose.

From this angle, the body is like a long log.

The ears extend outward from opposite sides of the head.

Draw in the fluff of the ears and tail. Then erase any extra lines.

— Flapping ears —

A flabbit can fly by gliding with stretched ears, or by flapping its ears up and down, like here.

HUMONGO FUZZ

The humongo fuzz is a giant, fluffy moth. When it flaps its wings, it produces huge gusts of powerful wind.

Instead of eating from tiny flowers like most moths, the humongo fuzz is so big it snacks on whole trees!

Start by making a circle for the head and an oval for the body.

Add round lines to make the tail, limbs, antennae and nose.

The last step is to add the giant wings. The top part of the wing is larger than the bottom part.

Open wings

When colouring the wings, outline the borders with a bright colour, like this yellow.

Add circles near the bottom of both wings to add another pop of colour.

Wings in motion

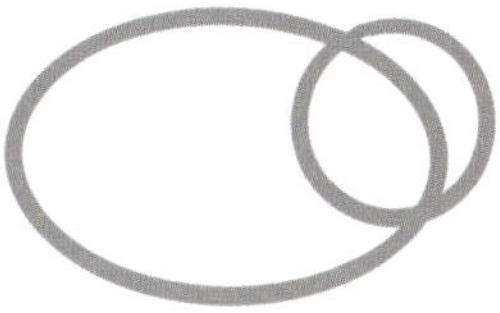

Begin with a circle and oval as usual.

Notice how the wings in this position are more curved, and echo the shape of the antennae.

Snack time

The placement of the head and body determines the pose of your creature.

The body is diagonal, so it looks like humongo fuzz is leaning forward to get stuck into its snack.

PTERADORKYL

The pteradorkyl is a dorky flying reptile with wings for arms and a cute nose. It has a friendly face and a personality to match!

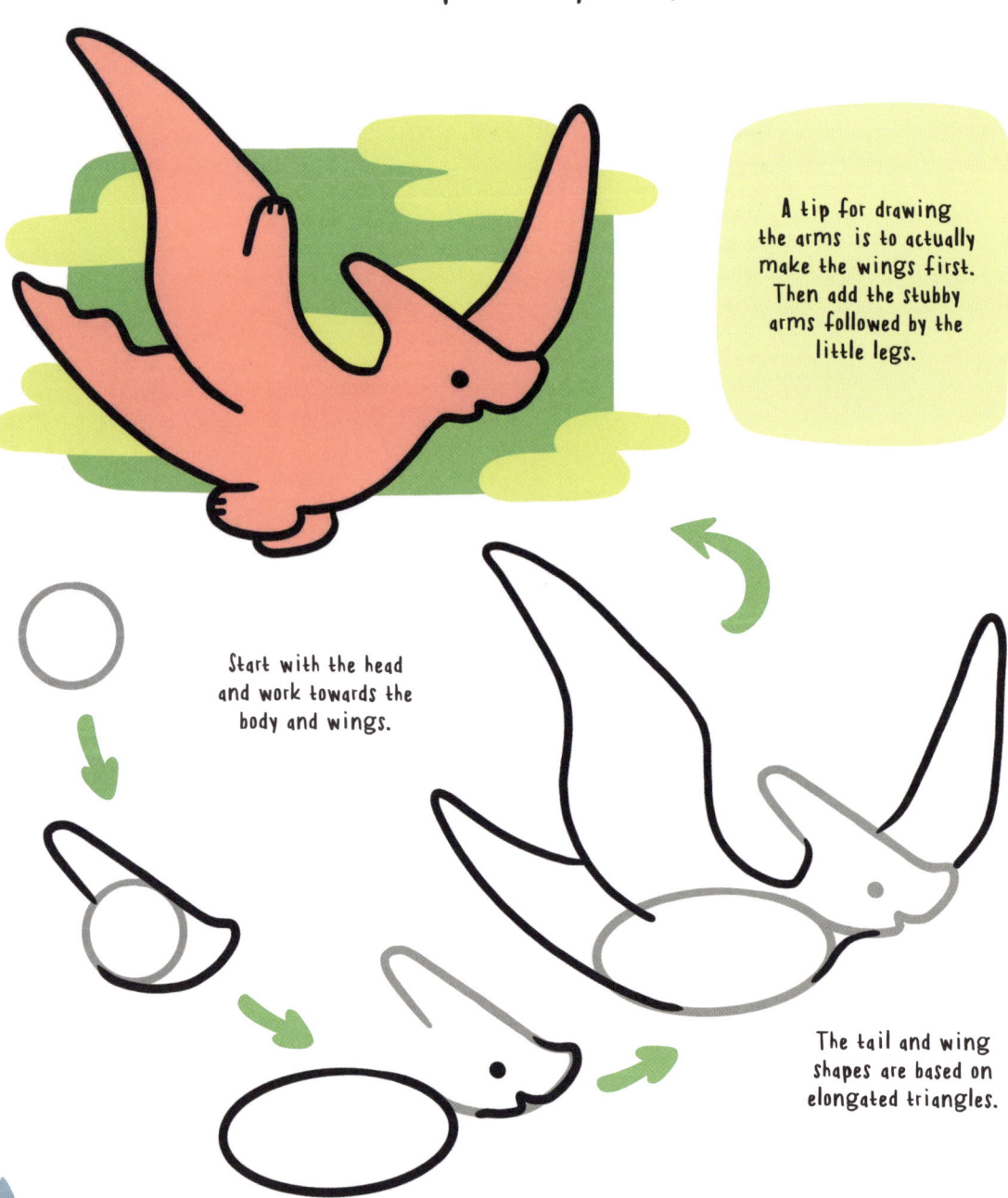

A tip for drawing the arms is to actually make the wings first. Then add the stubby arms followed by the little legs.

Start with the head and work towards the body and wings.

The tail and wing shapes are based on elongated triangles.

For dynamic poses, try drawing the pteradorkyl flying upward so you can see its tummy, or downward so you see its whole back.

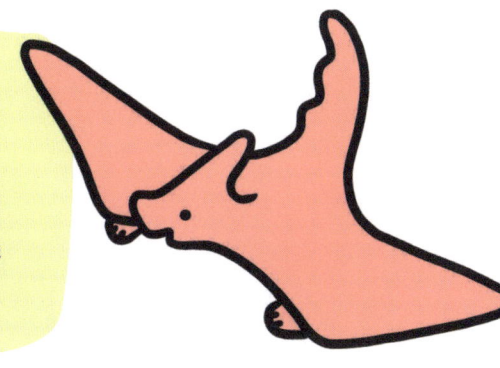

Sitting position

Draw a small and a large oval, and a slightly curved triangle for the tail.

Add in the details using shapes based on triangles and rectangles.

Finish off with the second wing and bumps on the tail.

Take off

Imagine the pteradorkyl jumping up when you draw this pose!

WINGEDEER

The wingedeer is a confident creature that likes to prance in the forest. It has a heart on its side because it has a lot of love to share.

The pinkish colours of the wingedeer look great against a purplish forest floor.

Draw the base of your wingedeer, which includes the head, body and limbs.

Next, draw on the fluffy tail and round wings.

The antlers are symmetrical, so take your time when drawing them.

Dashing

The body is a jelly-bean shape when the wingedeer is in dashing pose.

Draw the legs crossing in opposite directions.

Keep the head and antlers tilted forward while the wings and tail tilt the opposite way.

Soaring

Start with the head and body shapes and add limbs on one side only.

Add in the details, including the front leg on the other side of the body.

Draw the wings fanned out for the soaring pose.

Charging

Draw an upside-down jelly bean for the body.

For this pose, remember that the back legs are standing while the front legs are scrunched up.

Chapter four
LAND BEASTS

Cats, dinosaurs and even rocks and goop
make an appearance in the world of
fantasy land-dwelling beasts.

BASILISK

The basilisk is a large serpent that lives near rivers and forests. It enjoys cuddling with plants, like soft flowers.

Draw flowers around the basilisk to provide a setting for your drawing.

The spikes on its head are what makes the basilisk different from other snakes.

Draw a circle for the head, and a wavy line to begin the body.

Add another wavy line to fill out the rest of the body.

In a knot

This pose looks similar to a letter 'S'.

The tail crosses over the back of the basilisk, creating a small knotted curve in the body.

Snout and spikes

Always start with the head and work downward to the tail.

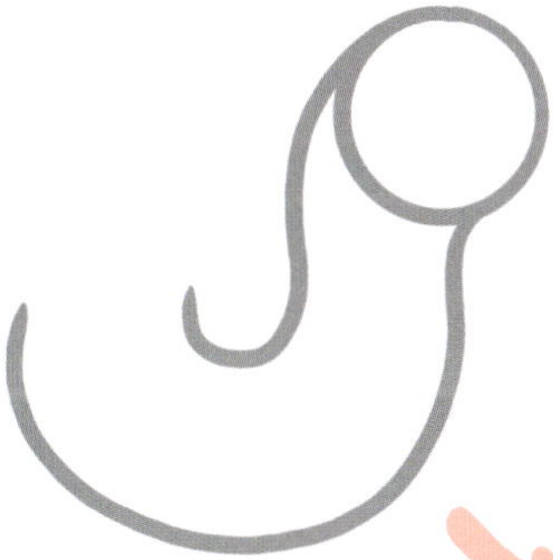

The basilisk has a cute snout that makes its face distinct. Without the snout, your snake might look like a worm!

The snout and spikes on the head are similar in shape.

RHINO PUP

The rhino pup has a big nose to sniff out food near and far. It's also a horn that can be used to dig up treasure.

Add the pup's features around the edges of the watermelon base. The tail and nose curve upward. Make the nose slightly longer.

The body shape of the rhino pup is similar to a watermelon slice. Make the edges soft and round.

A little rest

When the rhino pup is resting, its legs lie flat beside its body.

Sniffing out a snack

The rhino pup is a herbivore, so it likes to munch on grass and other plants.

From the front view, the rhino pup is made up of circles instead of the watermelon shape.

The nose is still a curved triangle. And the ear is like a teardrop.

FIRE PUPPER

The fire pupper is brave and adventurous. When it runs, flames erupt from its body, so you need to be careful when you play with this puppy!

Use one colour for the main body and a different colour for the wavy, flamy fur.

Draw circles for the head and body, and cute little triangles for the ears.

Add the limbs and facial features, then little wavy lines to create the flames around the legs and face.

Heroic look

The fire pupper looks similar to a cat to start with.

Drawing in the snout makes it look less like a cat.

Running with flames

The tail starts out like an oval triangle.

Draw a round snout for the side profile.

Add a wavy shape to the tail and little flames shooting out nearby.

Elegant resting

To make the fire pupper look like it's lying down, draw the limbs closer to the body.

Fire pupper

PLUMASAUR

The plumasaur is a scaly reptile with feathers on its back. It can walk on its two strong back legs, or crawl using all four legs.

To begin, draw two ovals. Notice how the head is more rectangular than the body.

Start forming the outlines of the plumasaur by drawing around the original ovals.

Draw in the legs. For the feathers, repeat the same loop shape but change the size.

Scavenging for food

The plumasaur crawls close to the ground to look for food. It uses its front limbs to dig up insects hiding in the dirt.

Angry roar

Add an eyebrow to show that the plumasaur is angry!

This pose has a slightly complicated base with quite a few shapes. Draw the head first and work down towards the body.

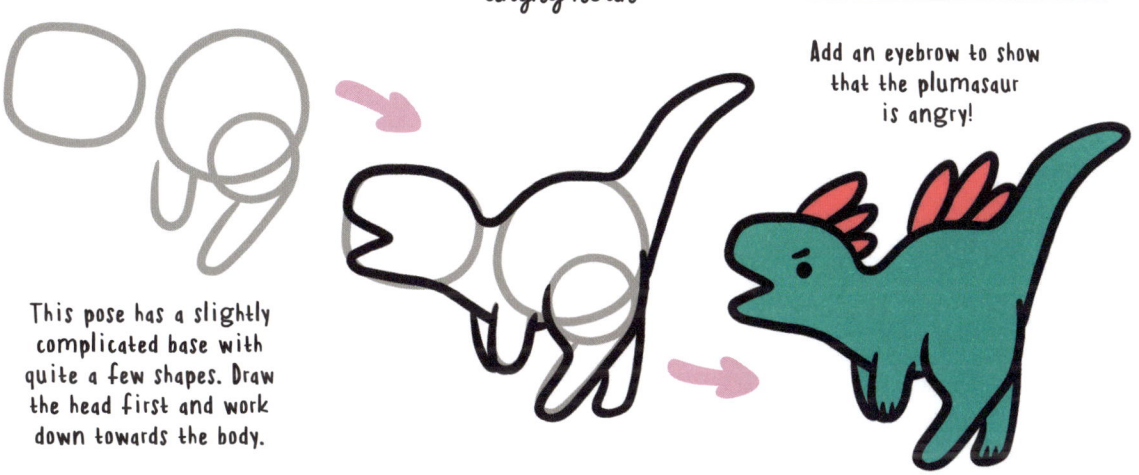

Saying hello

Use the same shape for the head as usual, but add the mouth on the other side to show the plumasaur is looking back.

UNICORN

People often talk about how beautiful and rare unicorns are, but no one mentions how clever they are! Of all the cute beasts, it's the unicorn you'll want on your quiz team.

Start with a circle for the head and a jelly-bean shape for the body. Don't forget the horn!

Continue to draw in the mane and front legs.

Add the back legs and details to the horn.

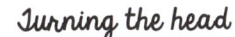

Draw the unicorn's mane in the same direction as its neck. The lines for the mane and neck almost run parallel.

To make a dynamic pose, draw the unicorn's head facing its body.

— A powerful stance —

The snout of the unicorn is like a semicircle. Erase any extra lines you don't need later.

SKULL PUPPY

The skull puppy is a very playful, nocturnal dog. It has bone armour on its face and legs for protection.

As is the case for most animals, start by drawing circles for the puppy's head and body.

Imagine that the pieces of armour are eggs, and draw them above the limbs.

Playing around

The pouncing pose starts with the body higher than the head.

The skull puppy loves to play by rolling around and pouncing!

Draw in the fur, ears and armour.

Add fangs to the face, and don't forget the paw lines.

Chilling time

One of the front legs is bent while the other is straight.

Continue drawing on top of the base by adding the tail and armour.

Sometimes the skull puppy just needs to rest.

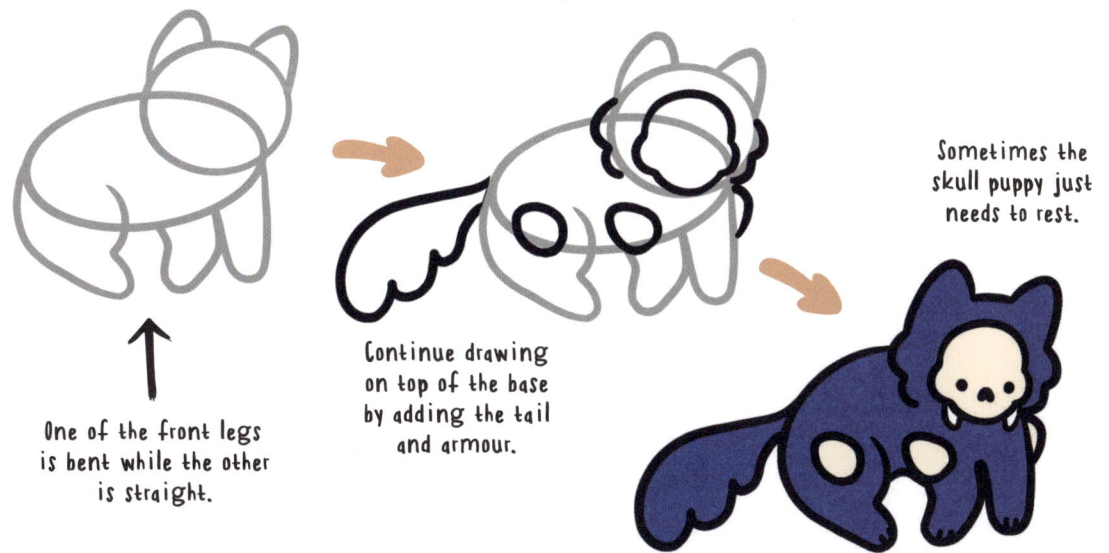

Skull puppy

LERRY

The lerry is a giant horned creature that roams the mountains. Its body is very large, so it moves very slowly. Slow and steady wins the race!

Despite the lerry being a warm colour, it spends most of its time in the cold mountains.

The head, body and legs are all rounded rectangles . . .

. . . while the horns and tail are triangular.

Charging forward

This is the front view of the lerry. Draw two rounded rectangles stacked on top of one another, and build everything else from there.

Battle stance

Use the body of the lerry to guide where the legs go. Add a circle head.

Draw in the horns around the circular head, and the facial features with determined eyebrows!

Walking with purpose

This is the start of a side profile view.

From this viewpoint all the horns are drawn closer to the top of the head.

Lerry **95**

ANTEON

The anteon is interesting because it looks like a deer but has a reptile's body. It hangs out near plants because eating them hydrates its scaly skin.

Draw plants around your anteon so it's always close to a juicy snack. These plants are like little hearts!

The antlers are almost the same length as the body!

Draw round shapes for the head, ears and body.

Happy walk

Add bumpy lines to the basic round shapes to create that reptilian quality.

Prancing

When the anteon prances, its two front legs move forward while the back legs go backward.

This time, draw the heart-shaped plants sideways to make it look like the anteon is dashing through them.

Grazing on plants

The anteon spends a lot of time grazing in order to get all the liquid it needs.

Anteon

CELESTIAL CAT

This cat's third eye is for looking into the fifth dimension. They say that's where all the lost toys are hidden.

Add sparkles around your three-eyed cat to make it look mysterious and celestial.

The cat's head is like a horizontal oval, while the body is more of a vertical oval.

Cat poses are fun to draw because they are made of wavy lines, like the limbs and tail.

Land beasts

All curled up

Whenever a creature is curled up, the body looks like a jelly bean.

You can choose to make the eyes a darker pink or black.

Pouncing position

Did you know that cats like to pounce for fun or when they are hunting? The celestial cat pounces when it sees one of the hidden toys.

Winking face

Since there are three eyes, draw one eye winking while the other two stay open.

ROCK FELLA

A rock fella is a little boulder, usually with moss and plants growing from its head. Rock fellas don't say much, but they make cute faces!

Adding little details like small lines and boulder marks really adds character to your rock fella.

The key to drawing rocks is to make round shapes more rigid, so add straight lines around your initial ovals.

The legs are like small, soft rectangles. Top off the head with moss and plants.

Every rock fella starts out with a simple shape, such as a square, triangle or circle.

After drawing the simple shape, make the edges round.

Add boulder lines and moss as the last steps in creating a rock fella.

SHIBARUS

A shibarus is a three-headed dog that protects the ghost world. It's three times better at playing fetch than any other dog!

You'll need four circles for your dog: three heads and one body. Add a couple of legs.

Draw in the ears, faces and a tail.

When you are near the end of the drawing, put in the fur and features.

When your shibarus
is facing to the side,
draw in a snout.

Colour in the eyebrows
and a cute pattern around
the mouths.

The shibarus has strong
back legs, which means
it can stand up and beg
for treats!

When your dog is lying down,
the body is more of an oval
than a circle.

Sleep eyes are
dashed lines.

FLORUS

The florus is a tiny, flower-sized critter with features in the shape of a flower!

The head is a large circle compared to the small oval body.

Draw flower petals around the sides of the face. The top of the head has two round ears, and the tail is a little flower.

Out for a walk

The legs are thin and triangular. When the florus is walking, make the legs on one side face backward while on the other side they reach forward.

Expressive ears

The direction of the ears should support your creature's facial expression. Ears up for a cheerful florus.

When the ears are downward and the eyebrows curve up, the poor florus must be feeling sad.

OTTREE

The ottree is a playful otter with leaves growing from its back. The ottree spends most of its time on land, but its leaves allow it to breathe underwater, so it is also a good swimmer.

Colour in the ottree with a bright brown for the fur and a forest green for the leaves.

Draw a circle for the face and a jelly bean for the body. Add a couple of ears.

Add the front paws and a tail to the jelly bean.

Draw leaves all the way down the ottree's spine.

Playing with leaves

When the ottree curls its body, draw a jelly bean and circle as usual.

Draw the leaves under the jelly bean, the legs in the middle and the tail curling upward.

Underwater poses

A playful creature like the ottree deserves dynamic poses! Play around with the direction of the paws to make it look like the ottree is swimming.

Lying flat out

When the ottree is lying on its tummy it's easy to draw the leaves because you're making the same shapes over and over.

ARMOURTAUR

The armourtaur is like a buffalo with armadillo armour,
which protects it from getting hurt by bullies.

First, draw a large
oval for the body and
a small circle for the
head. The tail is a
curved triangle.

Add the armour
next. Imagine it
like wavy hair.

Finally, add the
details of the
face and legs.

Standing up

Always start with the body
before you draw the armour . . .

. . . then wrap the
armour around the body.

Keeping warm

The armourtaur curls
up to keep warm in
cold weather. Start with
an oval body shape.

Draw the armour
wrapped around the
oval, all the way to
the tail.

Curled into a ball

In this pose the armourtaur looks
like a curled-up hedgehog.

SCALIA

The scalia is a reptile horse with a giant fin on its head. The fin keeps the scalia cool by shading it from the blazing sun.

The scalia is based on a horse. Draw the body like a jelly bean.

The fin is a rounded triangle.

Add details to the fin by drawing three semi-ovals.

Looking back

Shapes that will help you start your drawing are a circle, triangle, rectangle and jelly bean.

Don't forget to add a pattern to your scalia's back.

Running and rearing

Scalias are very similar to horses in that they enjoy running and rearing up on their hind legs.

A neat trick for creating a dynamic pose is to draw a semicircle for the body.

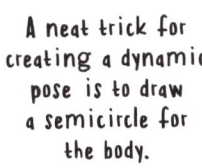

Add the legs to the opposite ends of the semicircle so your scalia looks like it's running.

Scalia ⭐ **111**

GOOP MONSTER

The goop monster is a slimy blob wrapped around a white mask. Since it is sensitive to the light, it has night vision and lives in a cave.

Draw a circle for the face and a big blob for the body.

Add squiggly lines around the body for the goopiness!

Draw ears and legs to finish your goop monster.

Boxy monster

First, draw a rectangle.

Draw just inside the rectangle to start forming the body of the monster.

Adding extra squiggly lines to the body gives it more of a goopy effect.

It takes all sorts

This goop monster has a bump on its back!

The goop monster can be formed from any basic shape, with added squiggles. Here are some examples of the different forms you can draw.

FLOPPY RAM

The floppy ram has large, curled antlers and small horns. It doesn't use its horns to attack, but it thinks they look like a cute crown.

Draw a large oval for the body and a circle for the head. Add the legs and a small tail.

Next, draw the large, droopy ears. Add small horns to the top of the head.

Draw in the curled antlers next to the small horns. Finish off with the cute face.

Leap into action

The floppy ram is about to leap! Make the front limbs higher than the back ones.

Don't forget to draw in the fluff of the body with bumpy lines.

Sleepy sheep

The floppy ram can snooze while sitting up, or it sleeps in a ball with its head down.

Taking a step

Lift just one front limb to start floppy ram walking.

ANTABUR

The antabur is a large, friendly bear with special antlers that grow out from its head and limbs.

Draw symmetrical antlers on top of the head and coming out from the tops of the limbs.

The antabur's base is made up of large circles and small semicircles.

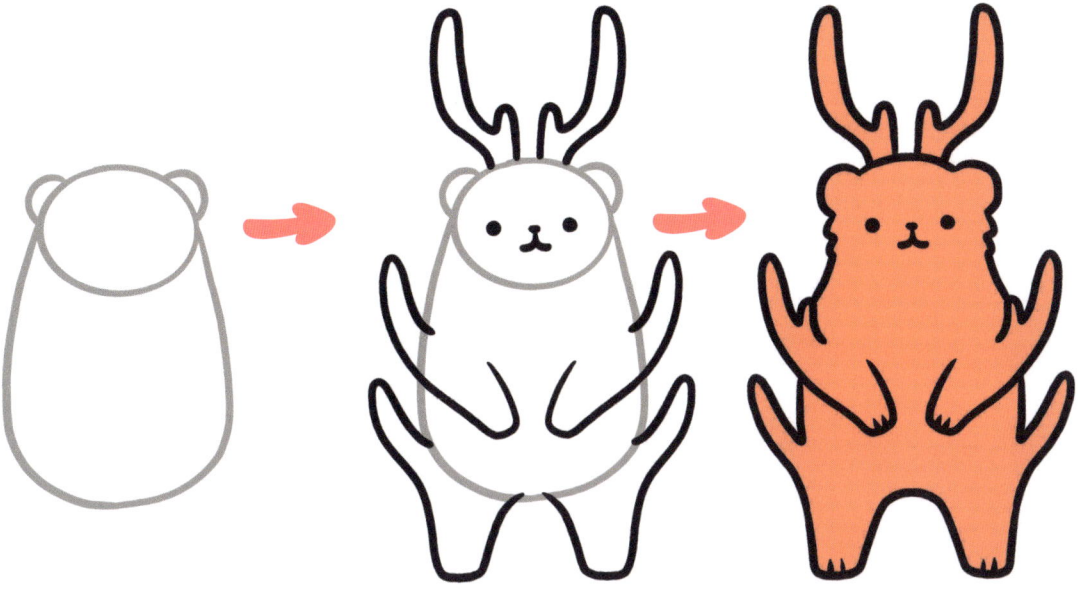

This is a fun pose to draw! Draw a large oval for the body, and a smaller one for the head.

Now for some symmetrical fun: draw one side of the antabur and do the same for the other side.

Add small details like the fur and lines for the paws before colouring your antabur.

— What to do? —

Some of the antabur's favourite pastimes are lying in the grass and eating honey.

HORNED TIGER

The horned tiger has a magical power: any plant that it touches turns a golden colour.

Draw in basic shapes like ovals and circles. The beginnings look like a simple cat!

Add the spiked cheeks and two curved antlers. Don't forget the tail!

When the tiger is sleeping, draw the oval body and circle head side by side.

Tuck the front legs under the head. Look how cute those small paws are!

Roaring into action

Angry eyebrows and an open mouth make the horned tiger look like it's roaring!

Sitting still

In this sitting position you can see all of the tiger's stripes. You can draw any pattern of stripes you like.

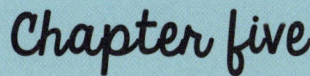

Chapter five

NOW DRAW
YOUR OWN

The really great thing about drawing cute
fantasy beasts is that there are no limits.
You can create a whole new creature any way
you want. If you need some ideas, let me
show you some ways to get started.

ANIMAL MASHUP

One way to create your own fantasy creature is by mixing two animals together. The best results come from animals that are completely different from one another.

Fish

+

Cat

=

Draw the first animal then start working towards the second animal.

On top of your sketch lines, define your creature with curved lines that connect the shapes together.

 +  =

Bats have big
ears and wings.

Foxes are land
animals with
four legs.

Keep the fox's body
while adding the bat's
wings and ears.

 +  =

Bunnies are
round . . .

. . . while snakes
have long bodies
and no limbs.

Use most of the bunny's
features and extend the
body like a snake's.

 +  =

Dolphins have curved
bodies and fins.

Turtles have a pointed snout
and rectangular limbs.

Combine the turtle's
snout and limbs with
the dolphin's body.

PLAYING WITH ELEMENTS

Each element has a special characteristic that makes it stand out. Here are four elements that can be combined with animals to create new elemental creatures.

Let's use a cat to draw out the different elements! Here is a simple cat with no elements applied. The fur is fluffy and a soft grey colour.

NATURE
Add plants, flower crowns, leaves and dirt for an earth-inspired nature cat. Plant colours like green and brown can add to the mood.

FIRE

Fire is intense and can be uncontrollable. Draw little flames everywhere and make the fur extra fluffy. Use combinations of warm colours like red, orange and yellow.

ELECTRIC

An electric vibe can be created with spiky fur, lightning sparks and bright colours such as yellow. Be careful! One touch and you might get zapped!

WATER

Water is smooth, wavy and transparent. This water cat has round lines and curved shapes all around. Use cool colours and white highlights to create a shiny look. Add sparkles to finish off the shine.

ADDING FEATURES

Another way to create your own creature is by adding additional features to an animal. Here are six different features you could try.

Wings   Patterns   Horns   Ears   Tail   Fur

Start off with a simple animal. Here is an outline of a dog.

Add a feature that a dog wouldn't normally have, like wings, or a pattern from another animal.

Complete the outline of your drawing and colour it in.

Dogs don't have horns or spikes. Draw on these new features to make a new animal.

Most dogs have fluffy tails. Adding a long and spiky tail can be a special addition.

Adding different kinds of fur or texture can change the look of your animal.

CREDITS

AUTHOR ACKNOWLEDGEMENTS

To my friends on Twitch, thank you for joining in on the art
streams and encouraging me to continue making art.
You are all so creative and it inspires me.

PICTURE CREDITS

Quarto would like to thank the following for supplying images for
inclusion in this book:

Abrym/Shutterstock.com; ju_see/Shutterstock.com; Oksana
Mashyntseva/Shutterstock.com; Marina Rich/Shutterstock.com.